W9-CKI-379

Pebble® Plus

Amphibians

Newts

by Molly Kolpin

Consulting editor: Gail Saunders-Smith, PhD

Consultant: Linda Weir
USGS Patuxent Wildlife Research Center
Laurel, Maryland

CAPSTONE PRESS
a capstone imprint

Pebble Plus is published by Capstone Press,
151 Good Counsel Drive, P.O. Box 669, Mankato, Minnesota 56002.
www.capstonepress.com

092009
005618CGS10

 Books published by Capstone Press are manufactured with paper
containing at least 10 percent post-consumer waste.

Library of Congress Cataloging-in-Publication Data
Kolphin, Molly.
    Newts / by Molly Kolphin.
    p. cm. — (Pebble plus. Amphibians)
    Includes bibliographical references and index.
    Summary: "Simple text and photographs present newts, how they look, where they live,
and what they do" — Provided by publisher.
    ISBN 978-1-4296-3989-7 (library binding)
    ISBN 978-1-4296-4852-3 (paperback)
    1. Newts — Juvenile literature. I. Title.
QL668.C2K65 2010
597.8'5 — dc22   2009023933

Editorial Credits
Jenny Marks, editor; Lori Bye, designer; Marcie Spence, media researcher; Eric Manske, production specialist

All diagram illustrations in this book are by Kristin Kest.

Photo Credits
ageFOTOSTOCK/Marevision, 15
Alamy/Juniors Bildarchiv, 17
Denis Radovanovic, cover
Dreamstime/Leyrer, 5, 7
iStockphoto/lesmcglasson, 1, 21
Visuals Unlimited/Gary Meszaros, 11; Patrice Ceisel, 9; Rob & Ann Simpson, 13

Note to Parents and Teachers

The Amphibians set supports national science standards related to life science. This book
describes and illustrates newts. The images support early readers in understanding the text. The
repetition of words and phrases helps early readers learn new words. This book also introduces
early readers to subject-specific vocabulary words, which are defined in the Glossary section.
Early readers may need assistance to read some words and to use the Table of Contents,
Glossary, Read More, Internet Sites, and Index sections of the book.

Table of Contents

Newt Bodies 4

Newt Homes 8

Prey and Predators 10

A Newt's Life 16

Glossary 22

Read More 23

Internet Sites. 23

Index 24

Newt Bodies

Newts look like lizards,

but they are amphibians.

They have damp skin.

Many newts have stripes

or spots.

Newts have long tails
and short legs.
From nose to tail,
most newts are 2.5 to 8 inches
(6.4 to 20.3 centimeters) long.

Newt Homes

Many newts live

in damp, wooded areas.

Other newts spend

their lives underwater.

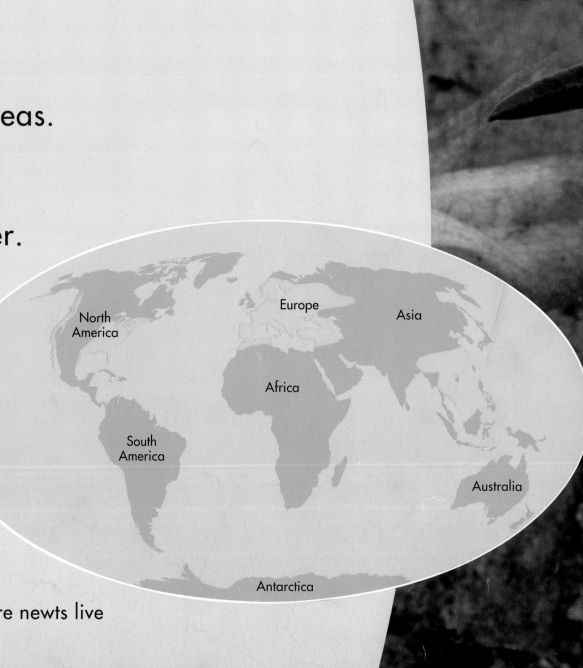

North
America

Europe

Asia

Africa

South
America

Australia

Antarctica

☐ where newts live

Prey and Predators

Newts quickly snatch up prey.

A newt's sticky tongue helps

keep its meal in its mouth.

Newts eat bugs, snails,

and worms.

Some newts have

bright markings.

The colors warn predators

that newts are poisonous.

Some predators

bite newts anyway.

A newt's skin tastes bad.

The predator may drop

the newt instead of eating it.

A Newt's Life

Newts lay eggs in water.

Many wrap their eggs

in leaves.

Some lay eggs under rocks

or on plants.

eggs

Newt larvae hatch

from the eggs.

Some larvae grow

into adults right away.

Other larvae become efts.

Newt Life Cycle with Eft Stage

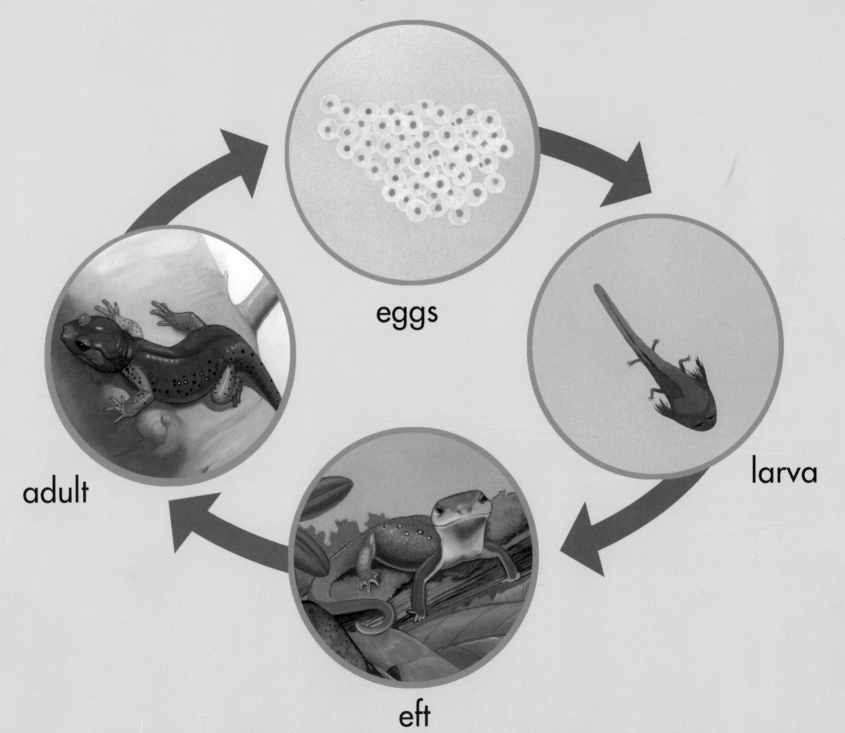

eggs

larva

eft

adult

Efts live on land

for three to seven years.

These young newts

return to the water

to become adults.

Glossary

amphibian — a cold-blooded animal with a backbone; amphibians live in water when young and can live on land as adults.

damp — slightly wet

eft — a young newt that lives on land before it returns to the water to become an adult

hatch — to break out of an egg

larva — a young newt that lives underwater; the plural form of larva is "larvae."

lizard — a reptile with scales, four legs, and a long tail

poisonous — able to harm or kill with poison or venom

predator — an animal that hunts other animals for food

prey — an animal hunted by another animal for food

Read More

Schulte, Mary. *Newts and Other Amphibians.* Scholastic News Nonfiction Readers. New York: Children's Press, 2005.

Snedden, Robert. *Amphibians.* Living Things. North Mankato, Minn.: Smart Apple Media, 2008.

Internet Sites

FactHound offers a safe, fun way to find Internet sites related to this book. All of the sites on FactHound have been researched by our staff.

Here's all you do:

Visit *www.facthound.com*

FactHound will fetch the best sites for you!

Index

adults, 18, 20

amphibians, 4

colors, 12

efts, 18, 20

eggs, 16, 18

habitat, 8

hatching, 18

land, 20

larvae, 18

legs, 6

markings, 4, 12

predators, 12, 14

prey, 10

size, 6

skin, 4, 14

tails, 6

tongues, 10

water, 8, 16, 20

Word Count: 164
Grade: 1
Early-Intervention Level: 17